# ANCIENT CHINESE PHILOSOPHY IMPACTS THE BUSINESS WORLD

John Curtis Newman

ISBN 979-8-89112-796-8 (Paperback)
ISBN 979-8-89112-797-5 (Digital)



Covenant Books
11661 Hwy 707
Murrells Inlet, SC 29576
www.covenantbooks.com

# DEDICATION

I want to thank the ALMIGHTY for the gifts he has bestowed upon me to create this work. I want to thank my wife, Renee Newman, and our five wonderful children, who never let me settle for less than my potential. To my parents for creating me and the life lessons they instilled in me. To my big sister Adrianne Burton and my brother Keith for having my back. To my Mastbaum family for keeping me on point with every endeavor I posted. To Coaches Derrick Tate, Derrick Norris, Michael Trout, Will J. Brown, Nasser Shine, Chuck Otto, and Frank J. Reinhardt, thank you for your guidance and support on and off the field. To my aunt Lutrecia Burton-Rhoades and uncle Wallace for seeing me for what I become and for not what I was. To my uncle John Burton III for reminding me of the legacy I have to uphold. To my late uncle Clifford Singletary for introducing me to *The Art of War*. To Victoria Myers-Fernandez for teaming with my wife to show me the way back to my potential. Last but not least, thank you, FB family, for all the support since we have been together.

# CONTENTS

# ACKNOWLEDGMENTS

Thank you to these writer s for allowing me to let them become a part of this book.


Al-Haris, Anis. "How Does Sun Tzu's *Art of War* Apply to Business?" Last modified July 26, 2014. Accessed July 17, 2017. www. Quora.com.

Bul-Godley, Elish. "Why Wall Street Loves *The Art of War*—a 13 Point Plan to Mastering Business Strategy." Last modified January 14, 2013. Accessed July 17, 2017. www.tweekyourbiz. com.

Cohn, Chuck. "How to Create and Maintain a Workplace Culture That Will Make Your Company Thrive." Last modified 17 October 2014. Accessed August 9, 2017. www.forbes.com

Delerue, Julien "Team Building: Sun Tzu *Art of War* to Build a Cohesive Team." Last modified May 17, 2017. Accessed August 14, 2017. www.1000meetings.com

Foo Teck Check. Interview 1999. Accessed. August 7, 2017. www. Sonshi.com.

Fox, Emily Jane. Interview with Dan Rather, "Dan Rather Explains Why Trump Is Smarter Than He Seems." Last modified January 12, 2017. Accessed August 16, 2017. www.vanityfair. com.

Graham, David A., "Would Sun Tzu Endorse Donald Trump's Total-War Political Strategy?" Last modified September 24, 2015. Accessed August 14, 2017. www.theatlantic.com.

Kuthiala, Puneet. "Sun Tzu on Loyalty." Last modified June 2, 2014. Accessed August 8, 2016. www.linkedin.com.

Laber, Justin. "This Week in Wrestling History: WCW Wins Ratings War Against WWE." Last modified June 21, 2012. Accessed August 9, 2017. www.bleacherreport.com.

Levine, Hallie. "Stick With It: 18 Fun Facts About the History of BAND-AID® Brand Adhesive Bandages." Last modified April 9, 2017. Accessed August 14, 2017. www.jnj.com.

McNeilly, Mark. "Six Principles of Sun Tzu and the Art of Business." Accessed July 19, 2017. www.suntzustrategies.com.

"What is a 'Non-Compete Agreement?' Non-Compete Agreement." www.investopedia.com. Accessed August 16, 2017

Pollitt, Chad. "10 Executive Marketing Lessons from Sun Tzu's *The Art of War*." Last modified July 2, 2013. Accessed July 17, 2017. www.relevance.com.

Revista, Roman "Sun Tzu—*The Art of War* Interpretation for Business." Artifex University, Bucharest. Last modified January 2014. Accessed July 17, 2017

Sun Tzu and James Trapp. *The Art of War* (New York, New York. Chartwell Books, 2012).

Sun Tzu. "Sun Tzu Quotes." Accessed August 2, 2017. www.brainyquotes.com.

# CHAPTER 1

# Art of War

How does the ancient Chinese military strategist Sun Tzu's book *The Art of War* impact the way companies run their operations?

The answer is the ancient Chinese military strategist Sun Tzu's book *The Art of War* impacts the way (1) companies run their operations, (2) build their businesses, (3) establish leadership, (4) maintain staff, (5) compete with rival companies, and (6) approaches indicative in such firms as Ford Motor Company, Oracle, Campbell Soup, and even the Boy Scouts of America.

*The Art of War* is one of the most diversely applicable books. The text was written by Sun Tzu during the Song Dynasty (960–1279) fifth century BC. Its contents are still being utilized and studied by many organizations, from football to educational institutes. Anis Al-Haris wrote about the correlation between football and the *Art of War* in his blog: "*The Art of War* has also been applied in the world of sports. NFL coach Bill Belichick is known to have read the book and used its lessons to gain insights in preparing for games" (Al-Haris, web). The intended purpose was to teach generals how to command the army while gaining the loyalty of the people and the trust of the emperor. In *The Art of War*, Sun Tzu wrote, "*Regard your soldiers as your children, and they will follow you into the deepest valleys; look on them as your own beloved sons, and they will stand by you even unto death*" (Tzu, Trapp, 67). The book is so profound that it is taught as required course content in leadership classes in many military academies around the world. The most noticeable impact can be found in the business world. Mark McNeilly expressed this in his web article "Six Principles of Sun Tzu and How to Do Business," "To find and exploit your competitor's weakness requires a deep understanding of their executives' strategy, capabilities, thoughts and desires, as well as similar depth of knowledge of your own strengths and weaknesses" (McNeilly, web). Many business writers have also written about the comparisons of *The Art of War* and business, like Elish Bul-Godley, who wrote the article "Why Wall Street Loves *The Art of War*—A 13 Point Plan to Mastering Business Strategy." In the article, she wrote, "The book states: before any steps are taken, research and planning are the key to any venture. My Interpretation? Any blueprint or business plan has to be compiled with reference to 5 basic points…" (Bul-Godley, Web). Chad Pollitt paraphrased one of Sun Tzu's famous quotes, *"The supreme art of war is to subdue the enemy without fighting.'* The most effective marketing doesn't even feel like marketing to the consumer." The ancient Chinese military strategist Sun Tzu's book *The Art of War* impacts the way companies run their operations, build their businesses, establish leadership, maintain staff, compete with rival companies, and approaches indicative in such firms as Ford Motor Company, Oracle, Campbell Soup, and even the Boy Scouts of America.

Many companies run their operations using lessons from *The Art of War*. One of the first lessons is establishing a culture. People who work in this environment, from the CEO to the janitor, work for the good of the company. When employees feel they are just as important as the owner, they strive to perform better. "They will always achieve your goals without your having to ask; they will be loyal without inducement and can be trusted to act correctly even without orders" (Tzu and Trapp, 75). The importance of having a certain culture brings all members of a company together like a family. "The skilled general leads his troops by the hand as though they were a single soldier, and they cannot help but follow" (Tzu, Trapp, 77). It is healthy for a company to be going in the same direction and working as one with two goals: success and progress. *"Personnel—* Maintain harmonious relationships between all levels of your hierarchy and create a unity within your organization that operates to an internal discipline. Ensure they get a *share of the "spoils"* to keep them motivated and help them buy into company Mission" (Bul-Godley, web).

# CHAPTER 2

# Blending Business

One of the authorities on the blending of business with *The Art of War* is Dr. Foo Check Teck. Considered by many to be Asia's foremost expert on Sun Tzu, Dr. Teck takes translating *The Art of War* to a different level. Dr. Teck has learned through extensive and in-depth research; he has established a global reputation. He makes the text "a living document" and translatable to the modern world. This is an excerpt from an interview he conducted with Sonshi.com:

I found many more CEOs and entrepreneurs, especially those who had to compete at the edge, are unconsciously applying Sun Tzu's *ping-fa* (transliterated as Law of Soldiering). That is a major contribution of my doctoral work done at the very ancient 1411 University of St. Andrews, a university where Prince Williams is studying. My PhD thesis was empirically grounded, using a large-scale database applying rigorous statistical analysis and across an entire ASEAN region. I surveyed top publicly listed corporations, including perceptions of the CEO, strategist, and top manager. That is found in Organizing Strategy: Sun Tzu Business Warcraft (selected by Blackwell in Oxford for Book-of-the-Month and then Spring's Choice). It is the very first study in the world documenting the relevance—metaphorically speaking—of *The Art of War* to strategic management of top, large, publicly listed corporations. There is, however, much more to my research (Foo Tek Check interview, web).

Company culture comes from the head of the organization. The company leader must have a strong moral compass and an understanding of the importance of leadership. "A Moral Compass bring the people into accord with the ruler so that they will follow him in and in death without fear" (Tzu, Trapp, 9). Chuck Cohn wrote in his article entitled How to Create and Maintain a Workplace Culture That Will Make Your Company Thrive:

> A great culture begins with the CEO and other leaders proactively setting the tone, and that culture permeates throughout the company when your core team sees this example being set. Your actions—and those of other important leaders within your company—help showcase the culture. Team members will likely notice if you do not "walk the talk," so it can be helpful to think of yourself and your leadership team as role models for the culture of your business. If you consistently present it in the right way, others will follow suit. Make sure you apply the same standards to your entire team when observing the culture in action. If someone puts forth a negative attitude or behavior that contradicts the cultural vision you have set, it is important to address it regardless of which role that person holds in the company. Take care to avoid giving special treatment to any level of your team, and encourage your core management team to do the same with their direct reports. (Cohn, web)

# CHAPTER 3

# Company Culture

The culture of the company is found in the product that people can trust and want to have. It is important to have a product that everybody wants. Put your customers in such a position that they will want to buy now then miss out later. If they feel it was worth the effort of not fleeing, then they will buy more. "Do not be afraid to send troops into a position from which there is no retreat. They will prefer death to flight" (Tzu, Trapp, 75). This quote translates into business planning. Pollitt paraphrased the quote, saying, "Sell something to a consumer and gain a customer today. Be truly useful or remarkable when marketing to a consumer and gain a customer for life" (Pollitt, web). Successful companies have used this ploy to make lifelong consumers. When your products are good, and the consumers trust the brand name, they will buy more. The best example is the Q-tip. This company made a name for itself, manufacturing cotton swabs. Q-tip has grown as a household name to such a degree that all cotton swabs found in stores are called Q-tips by consumers even though it's another company's product. Companies with strong brand names build local markets because loyal customers are close by. Companies use fewer resources in this regard because of word of mouth and free advertising. Local sports teams like the Philadelphia Flyers use this business tactic to grow their fan base not just locally but regionally as well. They use public relations to establish fans and garner support in other regions that generally support their local team. "A leader must understand the priorities of the local nobles before he can make profitable alliances…" (Tzu, Trapp, 81.) Another example of this is found in South Jersey. New Jersey is home to the New Jersey Devils, but the Philadelphia Flyers have a strong fan base there as well. How? Because the Flyers Organization convinced the city of Voorhees, New Jersey, to help build a training center there. This center generates money for the local economy, takes fans away from the New Jersey Organization, and grows its fan base for the Flyers. "On Home ground; don't waste too many resources campaigning here." (Bul-Godley, Web). Another way *The Art of War* impacts business is how companies build their businesses. "Use foreknowledge and deception to maximize the power of business intelligence" (McNeilly, web). It is also important to understand the overall nature of industry trends occurring around you to have a feel for the "battlefield" in which you will compete. "Be aware of markets or territories where your competitor has no presence and exploit these gaps" (Bul-Godley, Web). To keep your competitor from utilizing this strategy against you, it is critical to hide your plans and keep them secret.

"Know the enemy and know yourself; you will gain victory…" (Tzu, Trapp, 21). Many Forbes 500 leaders used this strategy to know the timing of when to take a chance on an opportunity.

# CHAPTER 4

# Timing Is Everything

Companies perennially found on the Forbes *500* understand that timing is everything in business. Knowing when to start a marketing campaign can make or break a company. "Opportunities multiply as they are seized" ('Sun Tzu Quotes," web). The best time to capitalize on the market is when the consumers have the money to spend. Consumers will only support your business when the market is safe, and great campaigns ensure that. Technology and consumer behavior are always changing and represent multiple marketing opportunities. Industry leaders know their market, and when consumers are at their peak, spending frenzy like Black Friday. "The goal of your business is to survive and prosper, you must capture your market" (Pollitt, Web). "In the midst of chaos, there is also opportunity." ('Sun Tzu Quotes," web). While that may be true in most cases, there are pros and cons to this in a frenzied shopping environment. An annual clearance sale at Walmart may not be a good time to introduce customers to a new brand. The positive customers will buy every bargain in the store while ignoring the new brand. Consumers are being tempted by a record number of marketing messages today that grab and keep consumers' attention. Great companies dare to be different and be helpful to the consumer. Consumers are one of two reasons companies find themselves in the best position to succeed. The other is knowing what your limits are by evaluating assets.

Most companies evaluate the best position of success by assessing their assets. *The Art of War* is like playing a game of chess. The rules of the game are predicated on the positioning of your pieces. Each move must be calculated and based on dictating the movements of your opponent. During the game, after you have taken a strong position, your pieces are ready to attack because your opponent can not move without giving away their position. The game ends when you can capture the king, or in business terms, their company. "In waging war, do not rely on the enemy not arriving for battle but on your own readiness to receive them, do not rely on them not attacking, rather be sure of the defensibility of your own position" (Tzu, Trapp, 51). If a company is running out of resources and is in a poor position, the company will have to abandon or drop out of the market and wait for another opportunity for success. Elish Bul-Godley enforces this with a lesson from *The Art of War*. "This phase, 'If *you know neither the enemy nor yourself, you will succumb in every battle.*' emphasizes Defensive behavior; securing and consolidating the resources you have and using them effectively as a solid base for exploiting new opportunities when they occur" (Bul-Godley, web). Companies that try to rush into bidding wars with other companies underestimate their own resources most of the time and lose bids because of poor leadership. "A general who is recklessly underestimates the enemy is sure to be captured" (Tzu, Trapp, 61).

# CHAPTER 5

# Strength of the Company

The need for strong leadership is an indicator of how strong the company is. A decision-maker must learn the tactics and strategies possible but especially needs to understand market psychology, use intuition, charisma, and resort to flexibility for teamwork. "Marketers who ignore the changing media landscape and consumers' ability to avoid advertising altogether are at risk of brand obsolescence" (Pollitt, Relevance.com). Sun Tzu wrote, "The general who advances without coveting fame and retreats without fearing disgrace, whose only thought is to protect his country and do good service for his sovereign, is the jewel of the kingdom" ('Sun Tzu Quotes," web). A leader who is fierce and is not timid to make decisions, especially involving expansion and financial gain, will be appreciated by the consumers, investors, and employees. "Don't be afraid to fail and don't chase influence" (Pollitt, web). It takes a special kind of person to implement strategic concepts and maximize the tremendous potential of employees. Sun Tzu describes the main traits of the preferred type of leader. The leader should be wise, sincere, humane, courageous, and strict. Leaders must also always be selfless and considerate, putting their needs behind those of their troops. It's a leader's character that gets the most out of their employees. Leadership equals quality, quality comes from trust, and trust makes the product easy to market.

"Marketing that is truly helpful to consumers is appreciated by them and positively impacts a brand's bottom line in perpetuity."

(Pollitt, web). Leaders must have trust from investors. Investors only give financial support when it is not costly to them and will not hesitate to intrude on dealings with business. Sun Tzu's strategy for dealing with unqualified businesspeople is, "Keep the other lords and princes in their place by harrying them; worry them and keep them busy; lead them on with hope of some advantage" (Tzu, Trapp, 51). This means having the ability to read the environment correctly and have enough foresight effectively based on the behavior of the competition, economy, potential customers, and even stakeholders. Finally, a leader must have in-depth knowledge of logistics. "Focusing on the Logistics of any plan and prevent over-extension of your company's resources" (Bul-Godley, web). "The line between disorder and order lies in logistics…" ("Sun Tzu Quotes," web). These two points of view are centuries apart, but their meaning is the same. A business leader must know what the company must move forward in any endeavor the company wants to pursue. Leadership will maintain a profitable and business-loyal staff that will work hard for management. "When troops are strong and weak officers, the army is disobedient; when officers are strong, and the troops are weak defeat is certain" ("Sun Tzu Quotes," web).

# CHAPTER 6

# Maintaining Staff

Maintaining staff is a key factor that *The Art of War* has impacted through business. The key components that are needed to succeed in business are honesty, strong policies, and respect for others. Being honest with the employees is a great start to keeping staff working for the company. "When one treats people with benevolence, justice and righteousness, and reposes confidence in them, the army will be united in mind and all will; be happy to serve their leaders" (Tzu, Trapp 9). LinkedIn blogger Puneet Kuthiala wrote, "Sun Tzu's *The Art of War* is a timeless classic, perhaps, to me, it is one of the best-written works humans have passed down through time. Whether it is read as it was meant to be, a war guide, operation manual in a competitive marketplace, or guideline to better help employers understand employees, it is a work of real meaning. Sun Tzu's *The Art of War* and its application in project management is tenfold. Sun Tzu was able to inspire big armies of soldiers to follow one great leader into battle based on 'Loyalty'" (Kuthiala, web). Having a strong policy will enforce rules and regulations that will keep the company safe and give a clear direction. "If, however you are too soft and do not establish firm leadership, too kindly and do not enforce your orders, if you are lax in your organization and cannot keep control—then your troops will be as useless as spoilt children" (Tzu, Trapp, 67). Establishing an informative human resource in the long way run is establishing responsible staff that can help people through tough times and answer questions on behalf of management. "Poor human resource management skills that utilize the wrong people for the wrong task, the inability to motivate your team or facilitate it" (Bul-Godley, web). Showing employees respect will keep employees from leaving to other companies. "Treat your soldiers like your children, you can lead them into the deepest, darkest places…"(Tzu, Trapp, 67).

# CHAPTER 7

## Guidelines to Compete

*The Art of War* gives guidelines on how to compete with rival companies. "His momentum must be irresistible and his timing precise momentum is the tension in a crossbow are and timing is the pulling of the trigger" (Tzu, Trapp, 29). If a product is selling well and the market is still intrigued, keep building on the product with new ways to sell it. When Apple introduced the iPhone on January 9, 2007, at a Macworld convention, it received positive feedback from the media attention. Steve Jobs, Founder of Apple, officially released the iPhone on June 29, 2007. The iPhone was so well received the company used its success to produce the iPhone series and to launch other products based on the momentum the company received from the iPhone. Being able to alternate methods generates momentum and ensures sustainable results (Bul-Godley, Web). As of today, the product line is on its eighth edition. Another product that has sustained momentum for a long period of time is the Johnson Family Company. This company has been around for more than a century and still produces products that people use today. The company started in 1886 by selling surgical bandages and adhesives. These were precursors to the product Band-Aid. Johnson & Johnson would later become the first company to mass produce the adhesive bandage with the help of Earle Dickinson, a cotton buyer and inventor of the Band-Aid brand adhesive bandage. The company became a major player in medical manufacturing, creating products like lotions, ointments, and their widely popular baby products and Listerine (Levine, web).

Identifying competitors' weak points puts any company on the path to success in defeating their competitors. "To find and exploit your competitor's weakness requires a deep understanding of their executives' strategy, capabilities, thoughts and desires, as well as similar depth of knowledge of your own strengths and weaknesses" (McNeilly, web). Taking the initiative to outdo the competition derives from this quote, "To rely on rustics and not prepare is the greatest of crimes; to be prepared beforehand for any contingency is the greatest of virtues" ("Sun Tzu Quotes," web). "The Western approach to warfare has spilled over into business competition, leading many companies to launch head-on, direct attacks against their competitor's strongest point" (McNeilly, web). This approach to business strategy leads to battles based on companies that have resources and the ones that do not, which ends up being very costly for everyone involved. Instead, the leader should focus on the competition's weakness, which maximizes the company's gains while minimizing the use of resources. This will increase profits and lessen their overall expenses. The leader should be aware of the company's operations and utilization of social media and the company's website. The leader must be their own personal spy. "Conversely, to keep your competitor from utilizing this strategy against you, it is critical to mask your plans and keep them secret" (McNeilly, web). Leaders cannot allow subordinates to know what they are planning until it's time to strike. The leader must gather all information possible, including stock prices, deals that are being negotiated on the competitors' behalf, and, most importantly, read résumés. These could become a great resource of information, especially if an employee left the rival company. They can give the leader viable information about how their competitor employs and how everyday operations are worked throughout the company. Companies that use "spies" generally get the desired effect they are looking for. "In this end, there are five types of spy you may use… Local spies are recruited from the enemy's peasantry, and internal spies from their court officials. Converted spies mean using the enemy's own spies against them.

Expendable spies are those who are fed false information so that it may be picked up by the enemy's own spies. Permanent spies are the ones who concentrate on bringing back reports" (Tzu, Trapp, 93). This type of "covert warfare" led to the invention of the noncompete clauses. According to Investopedia.com, a noncompete clause is "an agreement between two parties, typically an employee and employer, where the employee agrees not to use information learned during employment in subsequent business efforts for a set period. Employers usually insist on noncompete agreements because of the possibility of an employee, upon termination or resignation, working for a competitor or starting a business and gaining a competitive advantage by abusing confidential information about their former employer's trade secrets or sensitive information such as customer/client lists, business practices, upcoming products, and marketing plans" ("What Is a Non-Compete Agreement," web). These articles were established by businesses to keep former employees from going to rival companies—companies that stress the importance of loyalty. Successful business leaders take pride in their company being the standard all companies model their business after.

# CHAPTER 8

# Becoming the Standard

Positioning the company to be the standard requires alliances, mergers, and strategic control points in the industry to "shape" the opponents and make them follow the company's ideals. "Therefore, those skilled in war bring the enemy to the field of battle and are not brought there by him" (Sun Tzu, web). Engage pre-planned "strikes" on the competitors with product placement campaigns, thus gaining an early advantage and heavy share of the marketplace. Companies can obtain this by inventing the most innovative product, occupying new territory, or being the first to secure the marketplace. Once a company is in a position that dictates how its market works, it can begin to look at possible acquisitions. "The principles for campaigning in enemy territory are as follows: the deeper you penetrate, the greater the feeling of solidarity amongst your own troops, making it even more difficult for the enemy to withstand them" (Tzu, Trapp, 75). Utilize markets or territories where the competition has no presence and exploit these ventures. An example would be the WWE competing with WCW during the 1990s. WWE, during the late '80s, was the standard of wrestling. They had larger-than-life characters that young fans could cheer or boo. At the start of the 1990s, however, this was no longer the way to do business. Those same young kids were teenagers, and they wanted something new and a little bit more real. They found it in the rival promotion WCW. WCW was a wrestling company located in the South that was trying different ways to grow and outperform WWE. They found a way by acquiring wrestlers that no average fan has ever seen before. WWE, at the time, rarely went to these places for talent.

Before the internet was capable of streaming videos seamlessly, it was hard to watch wrestling from Japan and Mexico unless they were familiar with wrestling tape traders. The WCW company saw this as an opportunity to begin dealings with the smaller promotions and received an influx of new talent to blend with their established stars. Smaller regional companies like Ring of Honor and New Japan Pro Wrestling began stealing live audiences with their fresh stories, terrific microphone work, and exceptional wrestlers. After this business plan worked, the WWE began suffering, and from June 17, 1996, until April 27, 1998, they lost eighty-three straight weeks in the ratings war (Bleacherreport, web). When the WWE began faltering and in financial trouble, the company used the same tactic that WCW used to get better. The WWE signed a cooperative agreement with ECW, a Philadelphia-based company that was known for over-the-top violence. WWE used this venture to launch a new storyline entitled "The Attitude Era." Ultimately, WWE took over WCW and ECW and used their stars to enhance their company and set the standard for the wrestling market. "Take advantage of the enemy being unprepared; march by unexpected route, and attack where they are not fortified against you. (Tzu, Trapp, 73).

Companies that do not follow these guidelines or similar philosophies are going to be either bankrupt, taken over by a better-managed company, or sold. "There are pitfalls that may ensnare a general: reckless disregard for death will indeed result in death; too much regard for life will result in capture; a quick temper can be provoked into rash action; a misplaced sense of honour brings only shame; over-solicitude for the common failings causes needless trouble and anxiety. These common failings of generals and are disastrous in their effect on the successful conduct of war. When an army is defeated and its general slain, look no further than these five for the cause. They demand study" (Tzu, Trapp, 51). Companies fail financially because they do not pay attention to their partner's plans. "Do not enter into an alliance until you are certain as to the motives of your partners" (Bul-Godley, web). Companies that do not understand the process of victory falter. "In *The Art of War*, first comes scoping, then measurement, then calculation, then balancing and finally victory" (Tzu, Trapp, 25). Leaders need to learn the principles of project management. Project managers broker the deals that can elevate a company or bring a company down. They possess an awareness of the company's capabilities and surroundings, adjust the plans to suit the company's resources, and track or monitor the operations against possible deviation from the original plan. Most companies have used this assessment to enhance their own policies and principles.

# CHAPTER 9

# Principles and Policies

*The Art of War* fortified policies and principles in firms like the Boy Scouts of America. Sun Tzu's *The Art of War* translates well with the Boys Scouts mantra of "Always be prepared." The leadership guidelines prepare scouts to become leaders of their troop and trust in their training, such as using the surroundings as both food and shelter. The chairman and CEO Larry Ellison of the tech giant Oracle uses the principles found in *The Art of War* as guidelines to help his company grow, build, and produce efficiently. Larry Ellison, the second richest man in the world, is also a big proponent of Sun Tzu's principles, which are based on five ideas: philosophy, ground, climate, leadership, and methods. Ford Motor Company was built to innovate the car industry. The company uses one simple philosophy from the book that epitomizes its approach to innovation. "Never employ the same strategy twice, but use the infinite variety at your disposal" (Tzu, Trapp, 39). Campbell's uses text as a tool to keep employee retention high and employee turnover. Campbell's Soup Company uses *The Art of War* to stave off competitors with strong foundation guidelines and the importance of treating employees fairly. This explains why Campbell's soup company has had a low turnover rate and continued success through the years. Several human resource firms use *The Art of War* as part of their team-building concept. Directions Consulting provides sales training and team-building solutions for companies such as PwC, Evonik, Air Products, Air Liquide, Carrier,

Trane Climate Solutions, Bao Steel, AAM, 8Vale, Lenze, Duravit, Stanley Black & Decker, TNT, Texas Instruments, Dell, NEC, Epson, China Telecom, L'Oreal, Zegna, Swarovski, Yum!, Sinotrans, Johnson & Johnson Medical, Philips Medical, Invitrogen, American Express, Ping An Insurance, Axa Life, Bank International Ningbo, Malaysia Airlines, Starwood, and many more. Political writers even use the text as a barometer for the President of the United States. David A. Graham used *The Art of War* as a reference point to analyze what "Sun Tzu's *Art of War* have to say about whether Trump is toast. Two of these commentaries stuck out to me because in further gives evidence that The Art of War and business is a perfect match. The first assessment was based on the quote, "All warfare is based on deception" (Tzu, Graham web).

This is the most famous quotation from *The Art of War*, and it's one with which Trump, the businessman, would surely agree:

> "A little hyperbole never hurts," he once
> wrote. "People want to believe that something is
> the biggest and the greatest and the most spectac-
> ular... It's an innocent form of exaggeration—
> and a very effective form of promotion."

Trump, the politician, embroiders his own record shamelessly. His populist pitch, though, is built on a promise of honesty and openness. All these politicians play the game, he tells voters, but I'm the only one who's truthful about who I am and what I've done to play the game—and win it. As Tom Edsall writes, "Trump embodies precisely what his supporters say they hate—the exploitation of money and lobbyists to get his way. Nonetheless, he seems to have turned this to advantage by openly acknowledging how he has worked the system. His promise is to control the system on behalf of those who vote for him, rather than being controlled by it. Sun Tzu's Grade: FAIL" (Graham, web).

This was a sufficient grade based on evidence that Trump, at many junctures, has broken, bent, or rewrote the laws of business. When Donald Trump wrote *The Art of the Deal*, it was a game changer, but he tried to use the same antics, such as telling the people only what he felt they needed to know during his campaign. The public almost did not go for it. The secret to deception is secrecy, and because of social media, that led to his failed grade. Another assessment was how Trump handled his political rivals like Mark Rubio. The last quote introduced by the writer is, "If your opponent is of choleric temper, seek to irritate him. Pretend to be weak, that he may grow arrogant. If we wish to fight, the enemy can be forced to an engagement even though he be sheltered behind a high rampart and a deep ditch. All we need do is attack some other place that he will be obliged to relieve. So, in war, the way is to avoid what is strong and to strike at what is weak" (Tzu, Graham, web).

More than anything, Trump has shown his ability to pick a fight where it's most effective. Needless to say, he wasn't going to win a wonk battle with Jeb Bush. But by assailing Bush as low-energy, he found his opponent's weakness and has ruthlessly exploited it; Bush's standing in the polls has sunk consistently since Trump's entry (Sun Tzu's Grade: PASS, Graham, web).

The commentator believes Sun Tzu would have given Trump a passing grade on his ability to know when to fight and when not to. Trump has given pundits the impression he has never taken a stance that made him appear weak or clueless. Dan Rather said in an interview, "He's very selective on his facts, tried to delegitimize these new allegations that the Russians may have something embarrassing on him" (Fox, web). When he spoke at rallies, Trump mainly focused on building back up the financial infrastructure and job creation. He also addressed how weak the economy was based on the lack of help from the working class and the "failures" of the medical plan, OBAMACARE. It is a fact of business life to grow, attack the opponents' negatives when they try to be strong. Rather goes on to say, "We're reaching a point, very quickly, where he's got to deliver. These broad generalities—he will build a wall, repealing Obamacare and replacing it with something else—he's got to deliver on these things" (Fox, web).

# CHAPTER 10

# Clear and Present

"If words of command are not clear and distinct, if orders are not thoroughly understood, the general is to blame. But if his orders ARE clear, and the soldiers nevertheless disobey, then it is the fault of their officers" ("Sun Tzu Quotes," web). When CEOs or business owners give directives, they expect them to be followed by all personnel. To ensure that their directives and wishes are being followed, they lean towards supervisors, department heads, and team leaders to make this possible. When businesses are doing well, the praise goes to the head of the company and trickles down to management. Then there are cases when business is failing, but the head of the company is not at fault but the management they put in place. A prime example is found in sports. The owner of a franchise hires a coach who will help them win, and in turn, the coach hires coordinators and position coaches to make their vision possible. The position coaches train the players on the intricacies of their position. The coordinators work with the Head coach on the proper plays that would give their team the best chance to win. When a team wins and reaches their championship, opposing teams will see their success and want to hire those position coaches and coordinators to run their respective teams. However, when teams are losing, the entire staff is dismissed.

In the business world, the same rules apply. When businesses are run well from top to bottom, they are successful, but when a company fails, it's generally done because an owner will trust the people in charge to make great decisions that impact the future of their business. An example is Home movie and video game rental services giant Blockbuster Video, which was founded in 1985 and is arguably one of the most iconic brands in the video rental space. Blockbusters "thee" Friday night hangout for urban kids. Their slogan, "Make it a Blockbuster night," made weekends enjoyable for families to stay at home and enjoy the movies while at home. At its peak in 2004, Blockbuster employed 84,300 people worldwide and had 9,094 stores. Unable to transition towards a digital model, Blockbuster filed for bankruptcy in 2010.

In 2000, Netflix approached Blockbuster with an offer to sell their company to Blockbuster for US$50 million. The Blockbuster CEO was not interested in the offer because he thought it was a "very small niche business" and it was losing money at the time. As of February 2023, Netflix had 230.7 million subscribers worldwide, a revenue of $3.6 billion (US), and a stock market price of $309.32, according to Robinhood.

When companies do make good decisions, everyone wins. Microsoft acquired Activision Blizzard in an all-cash transaction valued at US$68.7 billion in January last year. The deal made Microsoft the world's third-largest gaming company by revenue, behind Tencent and Sony.

The acquisition included iconic franchises from the Activision, Blizzard, and King studios, including *Warcraft*, *Diablo*, *Overwatch*, *Call of Duty*, and *Candy Crush*, in addition to global eSports activities through Major League Gaming. According to Technologymagazine. com, the company has studios around the world with nearly ten thousand employees. This acquisition also made it possible to have exclusive content for its Xbox division that won't be available on other platforms. Microsoft is also looking to speed up the gaming evolution and accelerate the growth of its gaming business across mobile, PC, and gaming consoles, providing more jobs for IT technicians.

# FINAL THOUGHT

When Sun Tzu wrote *The Art of War*, his intended purpose was to teach military leaders about the basic principles and philosophy of combat and leadership. Over 2,500 years later, it has now become a requisite that any organization can learn from. Big and small businesses are using *The Art of War* as a how-to guide toward building a company. This text has taught leaders the importance of planning, organizing, maintaining, and expanding. *The Art of War* is a great example that knowledge can come from any source if it correlates with the information learned. The most intriguing aspect of *The Art of War* is how diverse the text is. *The Art of War* can apply to almost any scenario, whether it's football or cooking. People can learn different kinds of skills like team building, communication, and insight. Savvy businesspeople have built business conglomerates on the principles found in the text. Military leaders still regard *The Art of War* as the best source of learning how to defeat their enemies in a variety of ways. The text is without limitations. The book has been published with different interpretations of what Sun Tzu was writing, but this has always been the case for books at this level, like the Bible and the *Iliad* written by Homer. This creation by Sun Tzu has earned a place among the great written works that encourage people to be great leaders and rely on personal reflection to empower people and business enterprises.

# ABOUT THE AUTHOR

John Curtis Newman grew up in Philadelphia, Pennsylvania, attended public school, and received a degree in culinary arts from a community college in Philadelphia. He studied philosophy as a hobby, and it materialized into a passion. He studies the works of Aristotle, Plato, and Socrates. Once married, he started studying thoroughly the Sun Tzu classic *The Art of War*. Introduced to the book as a young child, he started applying the principles he learned to many of my activities, such as chess, coaching football, and cooking. He is married with five children.